THE ANCIENT WORLD

ANCIENT CHINA

BY LIZ SONNEBORN

CHILDREN'S PRESS®
AN IMPRINT OF SCHOLASTIC INC.
NEW YORK   TORONTO   LONDON   AUCKLAND   SYDNEY
MEXICO CITY   NEW DELHI   HONG KONG
DANBURY, CONNECTICUT

Content Consultant
Robert Bagley, PhD,
Professor of Art and Archaeology,
Princeton University,
Princeton, New Jersey

Library of Congress Cataloging-in-Publication Data
Sonneborn, Liz.
  Ancient China/by Liz Sonneborn.
      p. cm.—(The ancient world)
  Includes bibliographical references and index.
  ISBN: 978-0-531-25176-8 (lib. bdg.)
  ISBN: 978-0-531-25976-4 (pbk.)
  1. China—Civilization—To 221 B.C.—Juvenile literature. 2. China—
Civilization—221 B.C.–960 A.D.—Juvenile literature. I. Title.
  DS741.65.S67 2012
  931—dc23   2012005401

Photographs © 2013: age fotostock: 70 (Eastphoto), 75 (IMAGEMORE); Alamy Images: 94 (Adam Parker), 86, 102 top (Ancient Art & Architecture Collection Ltd.), 27 (Best View Stock), 14 (China Images), 84 (Directphoto.org), 35 (George Oze), 74 (Ivy Close Images), 36 (Lyndon Giffard Images), 68 (Panorama Media (Beijing) Ltd.), 93 (Paula Solloway), 19 (TAO Images Limited), 73 (The Art Gallery Collection), 95, 101 (The Protected Art Archive); AP Images/Imaginechina: 10, 11, 97, 100 top; Art Resource: 66, 103 top (Erich Lessing), 65 (HIP), 9, 62 (Réunion des Musées Nationaux), 13 (The Metropolitan Museum of Art, New York, NY), 29 (The New York Public Library); Bridgeman Art Library: 33 (Angus McBride (1931-2007)/Private Collection/© Look and Learn), 78 (Bibliotheque Nationale, Paris, France/Archives Charmet), 47 (Free Library, Philadelphia, PA), 50 (Free Library, Philadelphia, PA/Giraudon), cover left inset, back cover top, 3 (Indianapolis Museum of Art/John Herron Fund), 31 (Mogao Caves, Dunhuang, Gansu Province, NW China), 63 (Private Collection/Paul Freeman), 6 (Private Collection), 69 (Wang Xizhi (303-361)/© FuZhai Archive), 23 (Yan Liben (d.673)/Museum of Fine Arts, Boston/Denman Waldo Ross Collection); Corbis Images: 67 (Christie's Images), 59 (Royal Ontario Museum); Dreamstime: 91 (Gringos4), 5, 41 top (Jochenschneider), 24 (Lleska), 41 bottom (Mikhail Kokhanchikov), 49 bottom (Pat Olson), 71 (Typhoonski), 40 (Wenbin Yu); Everett Collection/Miramax: 96; Getty Images: 61, 64 top (China Photos), 60 (ChinaFotoPress); iStockphoto/Jorge Salcedo: 9 bottom; Library of Congress/Tui Bei Quan Tu, 1820/Chinese Rare Book Collection: 7; Media Bakery: cover right inset, 1, 28 top; Photo Researchers/Robert E. Murowchick: 48; Shutterstock, Inc.: 42 (Anthon Jackson), 28 bottom (aslysun), 55 (buriy), 64 bottom (igor.stevanovic), 81 (Jakrit Jiraratwaro), 85 top (johnfoto18), 85 bottom (Jump Photography), 79 (markrhiggins), 43 (stephen rudolph), 32 (Subbotina Anna), 90 (TonyV3112); Superstock, Inc.: 4, 15, 16, 17, 54 (DeAgostini), 25, 56 (Image Asset Management Ltd.), 82, 102 bottom (John Warburton Lee), 92 (Melvin Longhurst), cover main (MIVA Stock), 44, 89 (Robert Harding Picture Library), 80 (Steve Vidler), 38, 53 (TAO Images), 21, 30 (The Art Archive); The Art Archive/Picture Desk: 51 (Golestan Palace Teheran/Gianni Dagli Orti), 52 (Victoria and Albert Museum London); The Granger Collection: 12, 100 bottom (Ma Lin), 88, 103 bottom (ullstein bild), 9 top, 18, 22, 26, 45, 49 top, 72, 76, 87; The Image Works/Werner Forman/HIP: 58.

Maps by XNR Productions, Inc.

1 2 3 4 5 6 7 8 9 10 R 22 21 20 19 18 17 16 15 14 13

Gunpowder was first used in China to produce fireworks.

The oldest existing printed book is the *Diamond Sutra*, printed in China in 868 CE.

JOURNEY BACK TO ANCIENT CHINA

The many sections of the Great Wall were built over some two thousand years.

TABLE OF CONTENTS

An ivory beaker inlaid with turquoise, from the Shang dynasty

The Past Is Present

See for yourself how
ancient China is still present
in our lives today.

An ancient Chinese compass

THE WORLD PAN GU MADE

L ong ago, a great giant named Pan Gu slept within an egg. He grew so large that, when he stretched, the egg broke. The top of the egg formed the sky. The bottom became the earth.

According to ancient Chinese mythology, Pan Gu was the first living being.

Pan Gu remained between heaven and the earth. As he continued to grow, his body pushed them farther apart. After eighteen thousand years, Pan Gu was very tired. He fell asleep and died. His blood became rivers, and his body became mountains. His breath became the wind, and his voice became thunder. His eyes became the sun and the moon.

The people of ancient China used the story of Pan Gu to explain how their world was created. Historians define "ancient China" in different ways. But most commonly, it is described as the period from about 7000 BCE, when people in China began to farm, to 220 CE, when the rule of the Han family came to an end.

Today, we know a great deal about the ancient Chinese people. Much of this knowledge comes from written records. The earliest records were produced more than three thousand years ago. The creator of these written records carved a script onto bones and shells. Later, the ancient Chinese began writing books. In fact, one of the greatest inventions of their civilization was paper, which they developed about two thousand

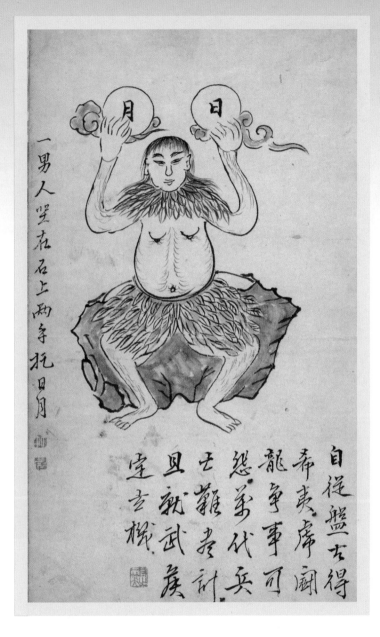

Pan Gu's body was believed to form five famous mountains in China.

This ancient Chinese writing was inscribed on the shell of a turtle.

years ago. Writing on paper enabled the ancient Chinese to keep extensive records about their lives and their beliefs.

Artifacts, or objects left behind by people long ago, are another source of information about ancient China. These artifacts include clay and metal pots, ornaments, weapons, and stone sculptures. Many of these objects were dug from the earth by archaeologists, scientists who study the distant past.

Many books have been written about ancient China. But the history of that era is far from complete. In recent decades, many new archaeological sites have been uncovered in China, often revealing objects that make scholars rethink their vision of this long-past world. In this way, our ideas about ancient China keep changing, growing richer with each new discovery.

artifacts (AHR-tuh-fakts) objects made or changed by human beings, especially tools or weapons used in the past

alchemists (AL-kuh-mists) people who work to make a potion that gives eternal youth or who try to change common metals into gold

AN EXPLOSIVE DISCOVERY

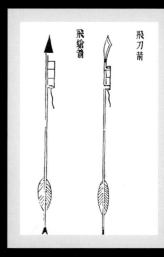

One of ancient China's most notable contributions to the modern world is gunpowder—and its discovery was a total accident! For centuries, **alchemists** in China tried to create a potion that would allow its user to live forever. One of the ingredients often used in their mixtures was saltpeter, a chemical compound known as potassium nitrate. In about 850 CE, an alchemist mixed saltpeter with sulfur and charcoal. The mixture had no life-giving powers; instead, it exploded with a blinding flash and a booming sound when it was exposed to a flame. The daring alchemist had unknowingly created gunpowder.

Ancient Chinese fireworks

The first uses of the deadly mixture included arrows with a burning tube of gunpowder attached to them, hand grenades, and land mines. Gunpowder changed the nature of warfare, affecting how battles were fought and how armies were used. It is still the basis for many modern weapons and is commonly used to make the fireworks you see at Fourth of July celebrations.

CHAPTER ONE

RISE OF AN EMPIRE

T he earliest humans to live in what is now China survived by hunting animals and gathering wild plants. But starting in about 7000 BCE, during what historians call the

Everything we know about the Neolithic period comes from the work of archaeologists.

砺石

Neolithic period, their way of life began to change. In areas with fertile lands, people began to practice agriculture. In the north-west, the primary crop was millet, a grass similar to wheat that produces edible seeds. In the south and southeast, rice was the main crop. With the rise of farming, people began to live in larger settlements. The largest were located near sources of water, such as on major rivers and along the southern coast.

These Neolithic people did not keep written records. But archaeologists have learned how they lived by studying the various artifacts they left behind. For instance, late Neolithic people living along the Yellow and Wei Rivers are known for their painted pottery. Late Neolithic people on the east coast produced black ceramics and decorative items made from jade, a hard blue-green stone.

Artifacts from the Neolithic period show how prehistoric people lived in ancient China.

THE XIA DYNASTY

Legend claims that about four thousand years ago, the people of what is now northern China came under the rule of a series of kings. The second to last was Shun. Instead of passing power on to his son, Shun chose a man named Yu as his **successor** because he thought Yu would be the better ruler.

Yu had already become famous for controlling the waters of the Yellow River at Shun's request. When the river flooded, it threatened to destroy the farms and homes situated along the waterway. Supposedly, Yu himself spent thirteen years digging canals to redirect the floodwaters away from the homes and farms. Another fantastic tale about Yu was that he could turn into a bear. Once, when his wife saw him in his bear form, she became so terrified that she turned to stone. When Yu called on her to give him a son, the stone broke, revealing a boy named Qi.

After Yu died, a leader named Yi succeeded him. Some accounts say that Yi willingly turned China over to Qi, the next ruler, while others claim that Qi had Yi killed. Despite what really happened, control of China would be passed down to Yu's **descendants** for a total of about seventeen generations. These men were the rulers of the Xia **dynasty**.

According to legend, Yu the Great was the founder of the Xia dynasty.

The Book of Documents, a collection of records made during the Zhou dynasty several hundred years later, includes an account of the Xia. However, there are no written records from the time when they were supposed to have ruled. Many modern historians believe that ancient stories about the Xia are nothing but made-up legends. Recently, however, some scholars have come to believe that the Xia dynasty actually existed. They think a few recently **excavated** archaeological sites hold the remains of Xia settlements.

THE SHANG PERIOD

Although it is not certain whether Xia was real or legendary, the next dynasty, the Shang, was real. The Shang (ca. 1600–ca. 1050 BCE) left behind extensive written evidence of their existence. Much of this writing appears on oracle bones, which Shang rulers used to predict future events. Oracle bones could be made from ox bones or tortoise shells. The Shang kings consulted oracle bones to find out about important matters, such as whether to fight a war or how to stop a flood. But they also used them to solve problems in their everyday lives, such as predicting the birth of a child or curing a toothache.

The Book of Documents *was created by scholars during the Zhou dynasty.*

excavated (EK-skuh-vay-tid) dug from the earth, often at an archaeological site

The Shang made oracle bones by either carving or painting characters onto the bone's surface.

The Shang carved questions they asked of spirits, as well as the answers they thought they received, on the bones. The carved **inscriptions** are written with characters that are close to the characters of modern Chinese. This shows that modern Chinese is descended from these ancient characters, making the Chinese writing system used today more than three thousand years old.

The Shang kingdom was centered on the fertile lands in the Yellow River valley. The kings and a class of nobles lived in towns and cities surrounded by walls to protect them from invaders. From about 1200 BCE, the Shang capital was Anyang, a highly populated city in northwestern China. Most of the Shang's subjects were rural farmers. Although the Shang had a regular army, the kings sometimes drafted farmers to serve in the military.

During the Shang period, people believed that gods had power over their lives. The living could not contact the gods directly, but their dead ancestors could. To seek help from the dead, people practiced ancestral worship. They performed ceremonies to honor their ancestors, during which animals and sometimes humans were sacrificed. The Shang also gave their ancestors offerings of food and drink. If the ancestors did not receive these gifts, they could harm the descendants who had neglected them.

Among common people, offerings were served in pottery. Offerings by the Shang kings and nobles were placed in metal containers. Metalworkers learned how to mix copper and tin to create a new metal called bronze, which was often used to make **ritual** vessels. Many bronze vessels have been found in tombs at Shang archaeological sites. The king's metalworking shops produced other bronze items, such as weapons and tools.

EMERGENCE OF THE ZHOU

To the west of the Shang kingdom lived the Zhou. Sometimes the two groups were friendly, but other times they were in conflict. During the eleventh century BCE, the Zhou king Wu determined that he could complete the conquest of the Shang dynasty that his father had begun. In about 1050 BCE, his armies invaded and took control of the Shang's territory. The event marks the beginning of the Zhou dynasty.

During this era, many important

This ivory beaker, inlaid with turquoise, was found in the tomb of a Shang king's wife and dates back to about 1200 BCE.

developments occurred that still have an impact on Chinese culture. In addition to a continuing attention to ancestor worship, the Western Zhou period saw the development of new types of music and poetry. The Zhou also established a governmental bureaucracy, a system of officials who helped the king run the kingdom.

In 771 BCE, some of the Zhou nobles allied themselves with foreign peoples and took over the heart of the Zhou king's territory, the Wei River valley. They killed You, the last of the Western

Bronze vases created by the Shang were often patterned with intricate designs.

Like the Shang, the Zhou crafted many items out of bronze.

Zhou kings. You's son Ping left the valley and headed east. At a new capital, near present-day Luoyang, he reestablished the Zhou dynasty. Ping and his successors, however, were never able to establish firm control over their eastern territory or regain power over their former kingdom in the west. The period when the Zhou capital was near Luoyang is called the Eastern Zhou period (771–221 BCE). Historians usually divide the Eastern Zhou era into two colorfully named time periods: the Spring and Autumn period (771–475 BCE) and the Warring States period (475–221 BCE). During the Spring and Autumn period, the Zhou kings struggled to keep their people united as various leaders challenged the kings' rule. In the Warring States period, these challenges grew more heated as seven states emerged and battled one another for power. Among the most powerful states were Qin and Chu.

This elaborate Zhou container dates back to the eighth century BCE.

As the fighting increased, armies of the warring states grew larger and larger. The battles they fought became bigger and bloodier. The Battle of Changping, for example, in 260 BCE, may have had tens of thousands of casualties.

Ancient China saw several positive developments during the Warring States period. The invention of the iron plow allowed the Zhou to dramatically increase the amount of food they could grow. This in turn led to a growth in their population. The constant state of warfare also had a positive effect on Chinese culture. Intellectuals came to believe that there was a growing disharmony between heaven and Earth. With the support of political leaders, many Chinese philosophers developed new theories about how to bring peace and prosperity to society. During this period, some of the greatest Chinese thinkers created philosophies that have had an enormous impact throughout the world.

THE FIRST EMPEROR

Between 256 and 221 BCE, Qin succeeded in conquering its rival states to gain control over the ancient Zhou territories and much more. The first ruler in the new Qin dynasty

was Zheng, who called himself Qin Shi Huangdi. His adopted name meant "First Emperor of Qin."

The First Emperor's most significant achievement was the creation of a Chinese empire. With the help of his chancellor, Li Si, he set up a central government and ended the fighting among the Zhou states. Under the First Emperor, China's new **civil service** gained importance.

The Chinese states sometimes battled using chariots during the Warring States period.

civil service (SIV-uhl SUR-vis) an organization of officials who administer a government's policies

19

Although the First Emperor ended the brutal struggle for power during the Warring States period, he was a very harsh ruler. He taxed his subjects heavily, often leaving them so poor they starved to death. He met all criticism with violence. Anyone who dared to disagree with him could be put to death. Scholars and philosophers were often targets of his fury. If he did not like their ideas, he had them killed and their books burned. The First Emperor is said to have buried alive about four hundred scholars he did not like.

THE HAN ERA

After the First Emperor died in 210 BCE, his son became the new ruler and took the title Second Emperor. Three years later, however, his subjects rebelled against him, and he was driven from power. The Qin dynasty (221–206 BCE) was destroyed, and ancient China fell into civil war as competing leaders battled for power. Liu Bang won the civil war and established the Han dynasty (206 BCE–220 CE).

The violence, however, continued as Liu Bang struggled to maintain control. His army was nearly defeated by the Xiongnu tribe living to the north. After Liu Bang's death, the empire remained unstable until the reign of Han Wudi, or Emperor Wu. Taking power in 141 BCE, Han Wudi established a strong central government just as the Qin had.

Han Wudi staged massive military campaigns that greatly expanded China's borders. He also increased China's trade network with central Asia. At home, Han Wudi was known for the academy he established for aspiring government officials. There, the wisest scholars studied the works of Confucius (551–479 BCE), a renowned philosopher of the Eastern Zhou period. Confucius

坑儒焚書

As depicted in this illustration from a later era, Qin Shi Huangdi was ruthless
in his elimination of thinkers who did not support his ideas.

This scroll depicting Liu Bang's victory in the civil war dates to the Sung Dynasty, in the twelfth century CE.

believed that, in the natural order of the world, subjects should obey their rulers. Confucius also believed that rulers should care for their subjects.

Many of the most notable thinkers in ancient China lived during the Han period, including Sima Qian, China's most famous historian, and Xu Shen, the author of its first great dictionary. The Han period also saw several important cultural developments. During this time,

Emperor Wu was the sixth ruler of the Han dynasty. This is an imaginary portrait of the emperor painted 700 years after his lifetime.

paper was invented, which allowed scholarship in China to flourish. The period also saw the growth of two religions—Daoism and Buddhism—that have had profound impacts on Chinese culture.

Although the Han dynasty lasted for about four hundred years, its emperors often struggled to retain their power. In fact, for

Many people today still follow the teachings of Confucius. In this picture, a modern artist imagines what Confucius might have looked like.

The ancient Chinese philosopher Laozi is known as the father of Daoism.

a few years in the early first century CE, they were replaced by the short-lived Xin dynasty (9–23 CE). Xian, the last Han emperor, was so weak that in 220 CE, he surrendered his post rather than fight to keep it.

The Han dynasty was over. But the **imperial** system established by the Qin and Han rulers remained in place. Emperors would continue to rule China until 1912, nearly seventeen hundred years after the fall of the last ancient dynasty.

imperial (im-PEER-ee-uhl) of or having to do with an empire

25

CHAPTER TWO

RULING THE REALM

Kings were the highest authority during the early dynasties of ancient China. The territory they controlled, however, was so large that they often had to hand over some power to high-ranking classes of nobles. In areas far from the capital, these nobles acted as the king's representatives among the peasant population.

Ancient Chinese kings ruled over huge expanses of territory.

As these nobles became more powerful, they started challenging the rule of the king. When nobles rose up against the king in 771 BCE, they acted with foreign invaders and assassinated King You. To justify attacking a king, a new idea about royal succession emerged. Called the **Mandate** of Heaven, it held that leaders received their power from a divine source. These leaders were entitled to rule as long as they were wise and good. But if they became corrupt and evil, Heaven would take away their power and replace them with better rulers.

Nobles gained more power near the end of the Zhou dynasty.

mandate (MAN-date) a command or authorization

FROM COINS TO CASH

The ancient Chinese were the first to use paper money. During the Tang dynasty in the seventh century CE, local governments began issuing it. Before paper, the Chinese used round coins with a hole in the middle. To keep the coins together, people strung a rope through the holes. But when a person had accumulated too many coins, the string of coins became too heavy to carry around. To lighten the load, the coins were given to a trustworthy

person. The owner of the money was given a small slip of paper saying how much money he had given to the other person. When the owner showed the paper to that person, he got back his money. Those slips of paper are now considered the first form of paper money. The idea caught on around the world, and today, in the United States alone, about 5.8 billion paper bills are produced each year.

The Mandate of Heaven encouraged ancient historians to describe dynasties as following a certain pattern. Early rulers were said to be great men, while the latter-day rulers were described as weak figures that Heaven was right to remove from power.

ORGANIZING AN ARMY

Highly developed organizational and management skills were required to maintain a large army. The state had to recruit soldiers and make sure they were trained to perform well in battle. It also had to feed and arm the troops. The government, therefore, had to make sure that farmers produced enough food and **artisans**

Artisans created weapons, clothing, and other necessary items for the Chinese military.

29

The First Emperor's victory at the conclusion of the Warring States period was only the beginning of his struggle to unite the states.

created enough weapons. The state also had to be able to assemble a large workforce to build protective walls to keep out enemies.

Future Chinese rulers learned several important lessons from the Warring States period. To discourage rebellion, a ruler had to make sure his officials were loyal to him. Should his enemies strike, a ruler also had to assemble his subjects to work together to defeat them.

BUILDING AN EMPIRE

The Warring States period ended with a victory for the First Emperor. From the start of his rule, he was faced with a challenge. The states he had conquered were longtime enemies. In order to keep new wars from breaking out, he had to somehow unite these states under one central government.

The First Emperor made many important **reforms**. One was to establish that the laws his government made would apply to everyone in China. Another was to create a standard written form of the Chinese language. This allowed people throughout his empire to communicate with one another more easily.

reforms (ri-FORMZ) improvements or corrections of something unsatisfactory

Improved roads made it easier for armies and merchants to move throughout all of China.

currency (KUR-uhn-see) the form of money used in a country

About a third of the Great Wall still stands today. It has been rebuilt and extended many times since the Qin period.

The emperor also made a single **currency** and standardized the system of weights and measures used in the empire. These reforms were meant to promote trade. No matter where the emperor's subjects lived, they could expect to pay the same amount of money for the same amount of goods. He also mandated that the axles of carts used to carry goods all had to be the same narrow size. This would allow them to travel on any road in the empire.

To further unite his land and people, the First Emperor launched an ambitious construction program. He sent out armies of workers to build roads throughout the empire. Eventually, more than 6,000 miles (9,656 kilometers) of roads were built. These roads made it easier than ever before to travel, even to remote areas.

The emperor also had laborers tear down old defensive walls surrounding towns and cities. At the same time, he started the construction of an enormous stone and earth barrier along the

Supervisors oversaw the vast numbers of workers who helped to construct the Great Wall.

33

northern reaches of his territory. The barrier was intended to stop the invasions of tribes to the north. Known as the Great Wall, it was built over a period of two thousand years. It is the longest structure ever erected on Earth. In total, the Great Wall stretches for roughly 5,500 miles (8,850 km).

A HARSH RULER

One of the biggest influences on the First Emperor was Han Fei. Han Fei followed a political philosophy then called the School of Law. These ideas later became known as Legalism. This philosophy taught that people are evil by nature. The only reason they will obey laws is to avoid punishment. Therefore, a wise ruler needed to severely punish any lawbreaker. Under the First Emperor, people guilty of even minor crimes were often put to death.

The First Emperor organized his people into the occupations most needed for government service—farming, construction, and the military—and taxed his subjects heavily. Some people paid in money or in grain. Others paid with their labor by serving in the army or working on the emperor's construction projects. The building of the Great Wall, for example, is said to have employed more than 300,000 laborers during the Qin era alone. Some were professional soldiers, but many were people forced to do the work against their will. Folk songs about the horrible hardships these workers faced are still sung in China today.

AN ARMY OF STONE

The First Emperor maintained a large army of flesh-and-blood warriors to protect China during his lifetime. But he also had a massive army of a different kind to serve him in the afterlife.

The terra-cotta warriors were arranged in actual battle formations in the First Emperor's tomb.

In 1974, a group of peasants digging a well discovered the First Emperor's tomb. Eventually, archaeologists unearthed about eight thousand life-size sculptures of soldiers. The figures, made from terra-cotta—a baked clay—were meant to protect the emperor after his death. They feature many different designs of uniforms, hairstyles, and facial expressions. The soldiers were originally painted bright colors, but the pigment wore off after being buried for two thousand years.

This tiny baked clay replica of a house dates back to the Han dynasty.

CHINA'S CIVIL SERVICE

The Qin dynasty lasted for only about fifteen years. But the strong central government the First Emperor created stayed in place long after his reign. After a few years of instability following the fall of the Qin, the Han dynasty took control of the government. During this era, the state developed a vast civil service that employed more than 130,000 workers. They performed services such as collecting taxes, storing government-controlled supplies of food, organizing building projects, enforcing law and order, and judging criminal cases.

The Han also established a new system of local government. The empire was divided into dozens of *jun*. These were areas administered by a governor who was assisted by a staff of military and civilian officials. *Jun* were further divided into smaller units called *xian*, each run by a local magistrate.

By the Han dynasty, rulers were suspicious of putting too much power in the hands of a noble class. Instead, they wanted loyal, well-trained government officials holding power. The early Han rulers sought out the best-educated scholars to work as government officials. Later, the emperors brought the most promising candidates for official posts to the capital for training in an imperial academy, which was established in 124 BCE.

Candidates also had to take civil service examinations. Only those who scored well on these challenging tests were given the best jobs. The very highest-ranking officials in the government enjoyed great status. Some were even allowed to marry into the royal family.

Long after ancient times, the Chinese civil service and the prestige of its workers continued to grow. In fact, the invention of the civil service is one of ancient China's greatest legacies. It helped rule imperial China for more than two thousand years.

CHAPTER THREE

A LAND OF PLENTY

In terms of area, modern China is the fourth-largest country in the world. Located in eastern Asia, it shares borders with fourteen countries, including Russia to the northeast, Mongolia to the north, and India to the southwest. China also has a long

The Kunlun Mountains stretch for about 1,250 miles (2,012 kilometers).

coastline along its southern and eastern boundaries. Stretching roughly 3,705,407 square miles (9,596,960 sq km), China contains nearly every possible type of terrain—from deserts to majestic mountains to tropical rain forests.

The borders of present-day China were roughly fixed during the Qing dynasty (1644–1911 CE). During ancient times, however, China's rulers controlled a smaller realm. The borders of ancient China also changed over time, depending on the current ruler's ability to conquer and control nearby territory.

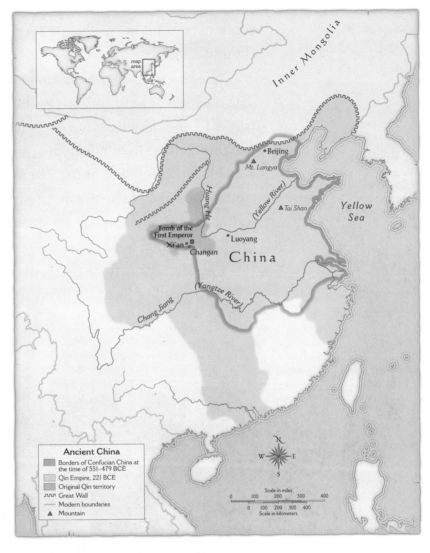

AN EXPANDING EMPIRE

The earliest Chinese civilizations were centered in northern China. The Xia, Shang, and Zhou dynasties ruled lands on the North China Plain. Running through their realms was the winding Yellow River. Measuring about 3,393 miles (5,460 km), it is the second-longest river in China. The Yellow River flows west from its origin in the Kunlun Mountains to the Bohai Sea. The Bohai is a gulf of the Yellow Sea located just east of Beijing, the present-day capital of China.

The Yellow River gets its name from its extremely muddy waters. The river is filled with soil eroded from the loess that covers a large part of China. This loess is a deep deposit of fertile soil that was carried on the wind from northern Asia many thousands of years ago.

After the collapse of the Zhou dynasty, the state of Qin took control not just of the northern plains but also of states to the south. Eventually, the empire stretched all the way to the shore of the South China Sea.

The Han dynasty further expanded the lands of unified China. It took control of territory in present-day Korea, Vietnam, and central Asia. The Han dynasty's lands also included the rich

The Yellow River is sometimes called the "cradle of Chinese civilization."

The Past Is Present
FINDING THE WAY

During the Warring States era, the ancient Chinese invented an early version of a magnetic compass. It consisted of a square bronze plate, on which a spoon-shaped instrument rested. The spoon was made of lodestone, also called magnetite, an ore of iron. Because this mineral naturally aligns itself with Earth's magnetic field, the spoon's handle would always point in a southerly direction. The ancient Chinese originally used their new invention to orient buildings and burial sites so that their location would be in harmony with nature. The magnetic compass allowed for navigation of the seas, which led to increased trade as well as to history-changing explorations and discoveries around the world. Magnetic compasses are still used by hikers, boaters, and other people without access to electronic direction finders.

The Himalayas are home to the tallest mountain peaks in the world.

region dominated by the Changjiang, or Yangtze River, in what is now southwestern China. True to its name, which means "long river," the Changjiang is about 3,915 miles (6,300 km) long. It is the longest waterway in China and the third-largest river in the world (after the Nile and the Amazon).

FARMING THE LAND

The regions along China's two great rivers provided ancient peoples with their best farmland. The crops that farmers could grow in each river valley depended on the climate, which was very different in the north and south. The lands on the Yellow River to the north were relatively dry. The high Himalayas blocked winds from the Indian Ocean, limiting the amount of rainfall the region saw each year.

The loess covering the area, however, made the soil very fertile. Deposits of fertile loess sometimes measured as deep as 250 feet (76 meters). In their rich fields, farmers grew grains such as millet and wheat. The farmers' harvests were plentiful enough to feed a large and growing population. But even in this fertile region, **famine** remained a constant threat. Sometimes, the annual rainfall was so low that crops failed. In the dry north, a **drought** could last for several years, leading to mass hunger and great suffering.

Vegetation flourished along the Yangtze to the south. The subtropical climate there was very warm and humid. Each year, the summer saw **monsoons**. These winds brought heavy rains and helped make the region ideal for growing rice. As farming techniques improved, more and more land was turned into rice fields. Eventually, rice became the most important food for all of China.

famine (FAM-in) a shortage of food causing starvation in a geographical area

drought (DROUT) a long period without rain

monsoons (MAHN-soonz) very strong winds; in summer they blow from the ocean, causing heavy rains; in winter they blow toward the ocean, creating hot, dry weather

The land near the Yangtze River is excellent for farming.

TRAVELING THROUGH THE EMPIRE

In ancient China, transporting rice to the north was difficult. China's major rivers run west to east, so there was no natural water route between the south and the north. In addition, although ships could travel the Yangtze, the Yellow River had long stretches that no vessel could navigate. The north and south of the Chinese empire were not linked until the Sui dynasty (581–618 CE), when the Grand Canal was built in the seventh century.

The Grand Canal eventually became the longest man-made waterway in the world, connecting the present-day cities of Hangzhou and Beijing. The canal helped transform China. It

The Grand Canal remains an important waterway in modern China.

encouraged the cultivation of rice in the south because the rice could now be shipped to northern markets. As more land was farmed in the south, its population grew quickly.

Road construction was also limited in ancient China. In the north, particularly, there was not enough stone to create paved roads. Instead, most roads consisted of ruts dug into the ground, through which the wheels of ox-drawn carts could travel.

The Han dynasty, however, did pioneer the use of overland trade routes, today called the Silk Road. Along the Silk Road, caravans of carts carried goods across China west into central Asia and eastern Europe. Dotted along the way were towns, where merchants could rest during their long journey. The road was a complex system of many trade routes. It owes its modern name to China's most important export at the time—the soft woven fabric called silk. Chinese silk was a luxury greatly prized by other peoples. In fact, the Han emperors used silk to buy off some of their most hostile neighbors!

Rice farming became a major part of the Chinese economy.

CHAPTER FOUR

LIVING IN ANCIENT CHINA

Social class determined the everyday life of people living in ancient China. At the top of society was the emperor. Below him were nobles and civil servants. Beneath this wealthy class were Chinese laborers.

Scholars had the highest status because they could read and write, and often worked for the government as civil servants. Farmers were respected because they fed the Chinese people. Merchants had the lowest social rank. Chinese thinkers disapproved of merchants because merchants simply traded goods rather than producing anything.

THE LIFE OF A PEASANT

Most of the people in ancient China were peasant farmers. Their day-to-day life was difficult. They labored every day, sunup to sundown, working the soil on their small plots of land. Usually, these small farms produced little more than enough to feed a family. All members of the family, including children, helped run the farm. Some families owned their own land. Others worked plots rented from large landowners.

Peasant farmers made up the majority of ancient China's population.

All farmers struggled to make the most of their land, especially in the north, which often had too little rainfall. For many thousands of years, Chinese farmers used simple wooden plows and stone tools. Beginning in the Han dynasty, however, the iron plow and new irrigation techniques were introduced. These advancements allowed farms to become more productive than they had been in the past.

Even in years in which the harvest was plentiful, peasant farmers struggled. They had to not only feed their families, but also pay taxes to their ruler in the form of grain. Often, however, their crops were destroyed by drought or flood. The frequent flooding of the Yellow River could be disastrous. Families would lose their harvest, their homes, and even their lives to the raging waters.

The Chinese sometimes used bulls to pull their plows during the Han dynasty.

A UNIQUE TREATMENT

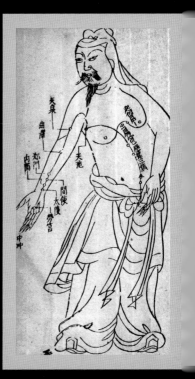

Doctors in ancient China used various methods to treat their patients. These included recommending certain diets, prescribing herbal medicines, and performing acupuncture. More than 4,500 years old, acupuncture involves placing long, thin needles into points on the body to relieve pain and treat illness. Ancient doctors believed that the needles affected *ch'i*, the life force that flows through the body. Acupuncture is still widely practiced in Asia today. In recent decades, it has become increasingly popular in Western countries, such as the United States and Canada. Many people, including doctors, question whether acupuncture actually works, although millions of patients rave about its benefits. It's currently used to treat many ailments, including arthritis, asthma, and severe headaches.

Ancient Chinese farmers worked hard for little reward.

FAMILY TIES

Family ties were very strong for both the poor and the wealthy in ancient China. Usually, several generations lived together in the same household. The eldest family members were treated with great respect by the younger ones. Elderly people, particularly men, were sometimes granted special privileges, not just by the family, but also by the state. During the Qin dynasty, men older than sixty years of age could not be forced to perform unpaid labor or be punished for certain crimes.

In general, men's favored position in Chinese life extended even further. Confucius held that just as people should obey the emperor, all family members should obey the male head of the household.

Outside the family, men also dominated public life. Men filled most public roles—from civil servant to philosopher to merchant. Women were generally thought to be inferior to men and were expected to submit to their wishes.

Neither women nor men were able to choose their own marriage partners. Parents almost always arranged their children's marriages. The bride and groom might not have even met each other before their wedding day.

Women were sometimes tasked with weaving cloth.

concubine (KONG-kyu-bine) a woman who lives with a man but is not married to him

In this illustration, a nineteenth-century artist depicts an ancient Chinese wedding procession.

The primary duty of wives was to give birth to children, especially boys who could carry on the family line. If the wife of a wealthy man did not bear a son, he might take on a **concubine** and hope that she would bear him a son. Men and their wives and concubines lived together, but a concubine had a lower status than the wife.

In upper-class families, only boys were educated. Girls, however, were instructed in singing, dancing, and sometimes reading.

HONORING THE DEAD

A Chinese family included not only its living members, but also its ancestors, including those long dead. Ceremonies to honor dead relatives were held on special days or on anniversaries of their death. The most honored were usually recently dead ancestors or those whose achievements had brought the family respect and admiration. Family members bowed to portraits of ancestors or to tablets engraved with their names. They also presented the dead with offerings of food, which the family later ate.

The ancient Chinese believed that people had two types of souls: the *po* and the *hun*. As the lighter of the two, the hun was the first soul to leave the body when a person died. At death, the son

Ancient Chinese were sometimes buried in carefully decorated coffins.

of the deceased person would call out for the hun to return. If the body did not come back to life, the hun was considered lost and the person officially dead.

When a family member died, funeral rituals ensured that he or she would pass on to the next world. These rituals had to be performed properly so that the dead would not bring misfortune to their living relatives. Bodies were buried with their favorite possessions. Wealthy people were often buried with hundreds or thousands of treasured objects.

Wealthy Chinese also invested a great deal of time and money in search of ways to extend their life spans. Experts advised them on diets, physical exercises, and breathing techniques thought to guarantee a long life. Because gold was a symbol of old age, the Chinese experimented with alchemy. They believed that if they could turn other minerals to gold, they could use that knowledge to create a potion to give them eternal life.

Funerary urns were buried with the dead.

FOOD AND DRINK

Most people in China ate a simple diet made up largely of grains, vegetables, and beans. In the south, rice was the primary food. It later became popular in the north as well, when transportation systems improved. In addition to millet and wheat, the northern Chinese ate a small amount of meat and fish, although these were rare treats for the peasant class. Throughout China, people used herbs and spices to season their food.

The ancient Chinese developed a system for cooking that used little fuel. They cut up their food in small pieces and placed them in a very hot pan, so the food would cook quickly. This style of cooking is still popular, not just in China but around the world.

For about five thousand years, the Chinese have been using chopsticks instead of a knife and fork. In ancient times, most chopsticks were made from bamboo. Sometimes they were crafted

Millet was an important food source for the ancient Chinese.

from animal bone, jade, and even metal. Chinese emperors favored chopsticks made of silver, which they believed could save them from being poisoned at mealtime. Tradition held that if silver came in contact with poison, it would change color.

Tea has long been a favorite beverage in China. The ancient Chinese used tea as a medicine and believed it was a key to good

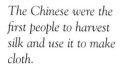

The Chinese were the first people to harvest silk and use it to make cloth.

health, wisdom, and happiness. Modern studies seem to support these centuries-old beliefs: some teas may help treat cancer and heart disease, encourage weight loss, and promote mental alertness.

CLOTHING AND ADORNMENT

Like most aspects of daily life, social class determined the type of clothing the ancient Chinese wore. Peasants generally dressed in loose garments made of rough fabric. Rural women usually wove the fabric themselves from fibers of the hemp plant and then fashioned it into clothing for their family.

Members of the royal court dressed in more comfortable clothing, usually made from silk. In addition to being very soft to the touch, silk was durable and easy to dye a wide array of colors. It was a particularly sensible fabric for clothing because it made the wearer feel warm in the winter and cool in the summer.

Producing silk, however, was an extremely difficult process. Silkworms produce silk filaments when they spin their cocoons. To raise silkworms, the Chinese had to cultivate forests of mulberry trees, whose leaves were food for the worms. The fragile cocoons had to be carefully unwound or else their silk would be ruined. Silk was produced in large quantities and was a favorite fabric of the wealthy. On special occasions, though, a wide range of people, not only aristocracy, wore silk garments.

The upper class of ancient China also used jewelry and ornaments to show off their elevated social standing. In early times, women adorned their hair with pins and combs made of jade, gold, and silver. Men wore belt hooks decorated with gold, silver, and precious stones. These ornaments were probably copied from ones worn by men of the Xiongnu tribe to the north.

Wealthy people often wore jade pendants such as this one.

Wealthy Chinese also adorned themselves with earrings, pendants, and rings. Jade was considered the most prized stone. Its hardness made it difficult to work with, so only specialists in jade carving could shape it properly. The Chinese associated jade with several important human characteristics, including justice, wisdom, and determination.

AMUSEMENTS

Chinese royalty enjoyed a variety of amusements. Singers, dancers, and jesters frequently performed for them. Jesters were comedians who sang funny songs and made jokes, often at the expense of the emperor and his friends. In quieter moments, wealthy educated people wrote poetry and practiced beautiful handwriting, called calligraphy.

The ancient Chinese also loved the circus. By the time of the Han dynasty, circuses were elaborate spectacles. They featured magic tricks, chariot races, wild animal hunts, and feats of strength. Acrobats were some of the crowds' favorite performers. These skilled entertainers awed their audiences by jumping through hoops, walking on tightropes, and juggling swords.

Games were popular as well. Many were played using dice or cards. For centuries, the Chinese played a board game called *liubo*. Two people played the game, moving game pieces in the shapes of dragons and tigers across a board that represented the universe.

Modern scholars are unsure of the exact rules of liubo.

Another popular board game was called *weiqi*, now known by its Japanese name, *Go*. Weiqi players moved black and white stones across a grid, trying to take over the most space on the board with their game pieces.

CELEBRATION TIME

Most of the time, hardworking peasants had little time for leisure. But for a few days a year, people throughout China put aside their daily work to engage in annual celebrations. The most elaborate was the New Year's celebration. Held for two weeks, it marked the coming of spring. Families would celebrate by cleaning their houses and holding a feast.

Today, the Mid-Autumn Festival is sometimes celebrated with elaborate fireworks displays.

In the fall, the Chinese observed the Mid-Autumn Festival, which is still celebrated today. The festival, which celebrates harvesttime, probably originated during the Zhou dynasty about three thousand years ago. It is sometimes called the Moon Festival because it is associated with moon goddesses worshipped by the ancient Chinese.

Qingming is a time for families to remember their debt to their ancestors. On this holiday, usually observed in early April, the ancient Chinese visited the graves of relatives. They swept the graves clean and left offerings of food, hoping to please their ancestors' spirits and thereby assure their own good fortune in the coming year. Modern Chinese people continue to celebrate the holiday today.

Many people continue to celebrate Qingming today.

CHAPTER FIVE

BEAUTIFUL OBJECTS AND SACRED BELIEFS

Since ancient times, Chinese artists and artisans have shown an extraordinary ability to create functional and beautiful objects. These objects represent China's rich cultural

This porcelain sculpture was designed to serve as a paintbrush holder.

Animals were a common theme in Chinese artwork.

heritage and reflect the Chinese people's ideas about religion and nature. Chinese art appears in many forms, including painting, silk work, sculpture, handwriting, and metal and paper creations.

Ancient Chinese artists used a wide variety of materials, including metals, clay, cloth, jade, and silk. The subjects of their artworks were just as varied, with a particular emphasis on animals, flowers, landscapes, and children. It is no wonder that ancient Chinese art has become renowned for its beauty and timeless appeal.

WRITING IT DOWN

During the Han era, the Chinese invented a new writing surface: paper. The first paper was probably made by soaking old rags in fluid until the rags broke down into fibers. The fibers were then placed into a mold, and the water was drained off. Once fully dried, the fibers formed a paper sheet. The Chinese soon began employing this technique to make paper out of other materials, including tree bark, bamboo, and rice stalks. In addition to books, the Chinese used paper to make kites, clothing, and even armor.

The invention of paper changed our world, allowing people to communicate and spread knowledge to all corners of the globe. People in the United States use about 71 million tons (64 million metric tons) of paper and paperboard, a heavy type of paper, each year. Amazingly, more than 2 billion books, 350 million magazines, and 24 billion newspapers are published in the United States every year.

FINE POTTERY

Pottery making is China's oldest art. Archaeologists have discovered Chinese ceramics that were made about seven thousand years ago. Different parts of China produced different types of pottery in prehistoric times. Pots made in central and northwestern China were shaped by hand. They are often decorated with painted designs. Some decorations are simply swirling lines, but others depict animals and human faces. Beginning in about 2000 BCE, potters on the east coast of China used the potter's wheel to make very fine black pottery with extremely thin walls. The black color was achieved by carefully controlling the atmosphere inside the kiln, or oven, in which the pots were fired.

Some ancient Chinese pottery is painted with simple shapes and designs.

Porcelain vases from the Ming dynasty are highly valuable.

As early as the Shang era, Chinese potters discovered a way to produce an attractive and durable glaze on the surface of a pot. The potters fired pottery made out of a certain type of clay to a high temperature and let ash fall on the pots while they were in the kiln. These ceramics were a type of primitive **porcelain**. Porcelain ware produced thousands of years later in the Ming and Qing dynasties are now considered among China's greatest treasures.

In ancient China, nonwealthy families used clay to make inexpensive objects that they buried with their dead relatives. The families believed the deceased would need these items in the afterlife. The items often included ritual vessels, cooking pots, and other household goods, as well as miniatures representing servants and animals.

BRONZE AND LACQUER

By roughly 2000 BCE, Chinese artisans had learned how to create objects from bronze. Their pottery-making skills came in handy while mastering this new craft. Artisans working with bronze first made a model of an object from clay. Once it was dry, they covered it with wet clay, which they removed and fired to fashion a mold.

The artisans then heated metal until it turned into liquid and poured it into the mold. When the bronze hardened, the artisans had a bronze object that looked just like their original clay model. Many of the most prized Chinese bronzes feature intricate patterns on their surface. Artists created these patterns by carving designs on the clay model before forming the mold on it.

Another art form that developed in ancient China was the use of **lacquer** to create lacquerware. Artisans found that the sap of the lac tree, when exposed to oxygen, became clear and solid. They

lacquer (LAK-kur) the sap of the lac tree used as a varnish

Some bronze creations, such as this vessel dating from the Zhou dynasty, were used for important rituals.

began coating wooden and leather objects with this sap to make them resistant to heat and moisture. Some artifacts are covered with as many as one thousand thin coats of lacquer.

Artisans also used lacquer for decorative purposes. They colored it with red and black pigments to give food containers and eating utensils a colorful sheen. Tinted lacquer could also be colored with various pigments and used to make painted designs. Because of its beauty, lacquer was sometimes applied to the coffins of Chinese nobles. For instance, archaeologists found two beautifully painted lacquered coffins, one inside the other, in the tomb of Marquis Yi of Zeng.

Lacquered objects take on a shiny gloss.

WRITING AND CALLIGRAPHY

During the Han era, the beauty of Chinese characters inspired the art of calligraphy, a style of elegant handwriting. Using a brush dipped in ink, calligraphers carefully painted characters, making each stroke in a specific order. A single character might require as many as a dozen strokes. Memorizing characters and the proper way to paint them required extensive training.

THE ART OF MAKING BOOKS

The first Chinese books were written on long strips of bamboo. One line appeared on each strip. The strips were tied

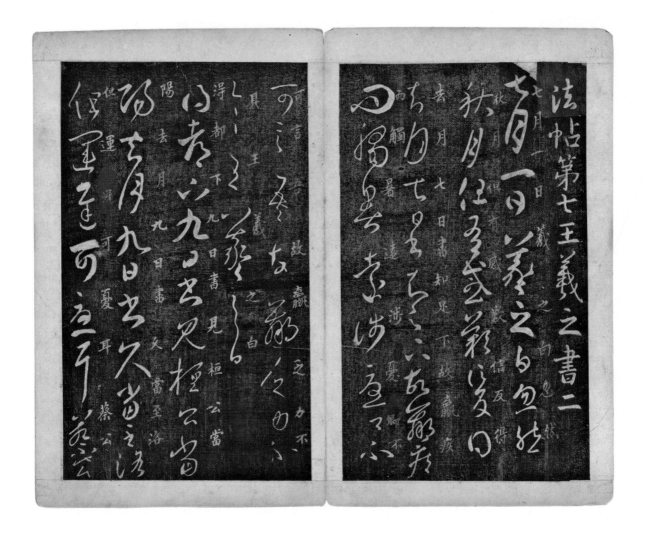

together with cords to make something resembling a bamboo place mat. It could be rolled up for storage and unrolled, like a scroll, to be read.

In some ways, bamboo was an ideal material for making books. It was very inexpensive. Also, the writing on bamboo strips could be easily scraped away, so the strips could be reused. When a book needed pictures, diagrams, or maps, they could be drawn on silk rather than on the bamboo strips. Silk, however, was much more expensive than bamboo, so it was used only for special purposes.

Calligraphy has been an important art form in China for at least two thousand years.

After their invention of papermaking, the ancient Chinese experimented with printing. They made some books by engraving text onto a stone, placing a piece of paper on top of the stone, and then rubbing ink on the paper to reproduce the text. This process was used for producing accurate copies of important texts, such as the works of Confucius, so that they could be widely distributed and read. Printing books from woodblocks was a later development. The oldest book in the world is a Chinese scroll printed in 868 BCE.

Bamboo books were convenient and easy to transport.

POETRY AND PROSE

The most respected literary form in ancient China was poetry. The earliest book of Chinese verse was the *Classic of Poetry*. Supposedly compiled by Confucius, it collected more than three hundred poems, ranging in content from tales about historic heroes to love songs.

Another important poetry collection was the *Songs of Chu* written by the famous Qu Yuan (339–278 BCE). Qu Yuan is said to have served in the court of Chu during the Warring States period. When he fell out of favor with the ruler, he was banished from Chu. While in exile, he wrote beautiful poems about his native land, which were later collected in the *Songs of Chu*. In 278 BCE, when Qu Yuan learned that Chu had been invaded by a rival state, he drowned himself.

Confucius may have played an important role in preserving China's ancient poetry.

*The strings of a lute
can be either plucked
or bowed.*

Later during the Han period, a new poetry style called *fu* emerged. A fu was usually a very long work. It included a middle section written in poetry, with an introduction and conclusion written in **prose**. These sections were often composed in a question-and-answer format.

In ancient China, works of poetry were not only read but also performed. They were often sung to music. *Classic of Poetry* listed twenty-nine different instruments played by Chinese musicians to accompany poetry. They included drums, bone flutes, stone chimes, bronze bells, and stringed instruments such as lutes and zithers.

In addition to poetry, Chinese writers wrote prose works on many different topics. During the Warring States period, for instance, military leaders produced manuals for fighting wars, including the famous *Ping-fa*, or *The Art of War*, by Sunzi (also known as Sun-Tzu). At about the same time, philosophers such as Confucius, Mencius, and Mozi explored questions about proper behavior and the ordering of society.

Writers of advice books instructed people how best to conduct themselves in everyday life. One notable book was by Ban Zhao (ca. 45–120 CE). Her *Nü Jie* (*Lessons for Women*) was a practical guide to how well-bred women should behave. Ban Zhao was also a historian of ancient China. After the death of her brother Ban Gu, she finished his book *Hanshu* (*History of the Former Han*), which chronicled the early rule of the Han dynasty.

Ban Gu's work built on *Shiji* (*Historical Records*) by Sima Qian. Written in the first century BCE, this work was an attempt to record all of China's previous history. While composing his masterpiece, Sima Qian had a dispute with the Han emperor Wu. Wu ordered a terrible punishment for Sima Qian, expecting the historian to commit suicide before it was carried out. But Sima Qian refused to kill himself because he was determined to finish his book. Thanks to the dedication of Sima Qian and his fellow historians, today we have a lively written record of ancient China told through the eyes of those who witnessed it.

Sunzi is considered to be one of history's greatest military minds.

Mencius believed that all humans were naturally good.

COMMUNICATING WITH THE GODS

Ancient Chinese writers are also responsible for telling us about the various gods that the Chinese believed shaped and controlled the universe. Like many early peoples, the Chinese told myths about these gods. The stories were not meant simply to entertain people. They helped to explain mysteries about the world, such as the origins of humans and the cosmos. One myth, for instance, told of a woman named Nü Wa, who molded clay to create the first human beings. Another featured two brothers, Shishen and Yanbo. Upset by their constant arguing, their father turned the siblings into constellations in the night sky.

Beginning in the Shang era, the Chinese came to believe that, if they made offerings to their ancestors, the ancestors would bring them good fortune. Many of the artifacts found at Shang and Zhou archaeological sites were used to communicate with these powerful beings.

During the Eastern Zhou period, upper-class Chinese began to question the relationship between humans and the natural order. Scholars disturbed by the chaos and conflict around them developed new ideas about life and how it should be lived. One of these schools of thought was

Legends say that Nü Wa created human life on Earth.

called Confucianism. It would have a tremendous influence over the philosophical and religious beliefs of the Chinese people.

THE WISDOM OF CONFUCIUS

Kong Zi, known to us as Confucius, served as an adviser to the leaders of Lu, one of seven states then fighting for dominance over

Confucian scholars carefully studied the teachings of Confucius.

China. He was also a teacher. It was in this role that he became famous. Centuries later, his followers collected his teachings in a book called *The Analects*.

Confucius looked back to the early, peaceful days of the Zhou dynasty as a golden age. He viewed that society as more stable and moral than his own. He saw it as a world where people showed proper respect to their ancestors and to each other. Confucius counseled his students to revive the virtues of that earlier time. He encouraged them to live an orderly life and strengthen their family ties, including their ties to their long-dead ancestors.

Confucius believed it was important for people to behave honestly and decently in their dealings with others. Such people, he said, had a quality called *ren*. In Confucius's eyes, only people who were ren should be permitted to perform important religious rites.

THE WAY

Another philosophy embraced by the ancient Chinese was Daoism (also spelled Taoism). This school of thought was inspired by a book titled *Daodejing* (sometimes called *The Way and Its Power*). According to legend, a man named Laozi wrote it, probably in the sixth century BCE. The short book contained many brief sayings. Much of *Daodejing* discusses the *dao*, or "the way," without actually defining what it is. Interpretations vary, but many readers think of the dao as a sort of mystical source of order in the universe.

Daoism emphasized the importance of living in peace and in harmony with nature. It also dealt with finding a balance between yin and yang, which the ancient Chinese thought were the two opposing natural forces. Instead of striving for wealth and power, Daoism told its followers to live simply and humbly.

Little is known about the life of Laozi.

reincarnation (ree-in-kahr-NAY-shuhn) being born on Earth again in another body after dying

Various religious movements based on Daoism emerged in ancient China. Zhang Ling, also known as Zhang Daoling, led the most important one. In 142 CE, he claimed he had a vision of Laozi descending from heaven. Zhang Ling then began a new religion that used Daoist principles to honor the old gods. He and his followers created their own state in a remote area of China. As the Han government collapsed, Daoism became the official state religion of the Chinese empire. By the later Tang dynasty (618–907 CE), Daoism had become such a powerful force in the government that its emperors claimed to be the **reincarnation**, or rebirth, of Laozi himself.

THE GROWTH OF BUDDHISM

During the Han dynasty, another religion was introduced to ancient China. The traders entering the empire on the Silk Road brought in not only goods but also ideas. They shared with the Chinese the teachings of an Indian prince named Siddhartha Gautama, also called the Buddha. Since the fifth century BCE, Buddhism had been slowly spreading through India and then East Asia and Southeast Asia.

The Buddha likely lived sometime between the 6th and 4th centuries BCE.

To many Chinese, some Buddhist concepts seemed very strange. For instance, Buddhists believed that desiring things caused people to suffer. If they did not overcome this desire in life, when they died, they would be reincarnated in another body. This idea, however, conflicted with Chinese beliefs about ancestor worship. If their ancestor's souls returned to Earth, as reincarnation suggested, how could they worship their ancestors in the spiritual realm? The Chinese were also disturbed that Buddhist monks were not permitted to marry. This made no sense to them, because the Chinese believed a man's main duty was to produce male children so his family line would live on.

Buddhist monks owned very few personal possessions.

Buddhists hoping to win over the Chinese had to find ways of making Buddhism seem less foreign and strange. They started using the language of Daoism to explain Buddhist beliefs. In this way, Buddhism as practiced in China became intermingled with this earlier religious tradition. In fact, to some Chinese, the two religions seemed one and the same. However, as more accurate translations of the Buddhist sacred texts were made, Buddhism in China became more faithful to the Indian beliefs.

Since the Tang dynasty, Confucianism, Daoism, and Buddhism have been called the Three Teachings. Each has played a significant role in shaping the ways the Chinese people of today think about the world and their place in it.

Buddhist temples are common throughout modern-day China.

CHAPTER SIX

ANCIENT TIMES IN TODAY'S WORLD

Even after the Han empire collapsed in 220 CE, its ancient imperial government and institutions did not disappear. In fact, in the centuries to come, the Chinese empire grew even greater in size and prosperity.

The Wei dynasty was the most powerful of China's preunification northern dynasties.

THE SUI DYNASTY

Immediately after the Han dynasty, China fell into disorder and confusion. Cao Pi of the Wei dynasty (220–265) called himself the new ruler of the empire. But in reality, China was now politically divided into three separate states. Wei was to the northeast, Shu to the west, and Wu to the south. As these states battled each other, a rival family managed to establish the short-lived Jin dynasty (265–316), which held power in the south. The north saw a series of local dynasties take power during what is now called the Six Dynasties era.

In 581, this chaotic period came to an end when the Sui took control over the entire empire. The Sui dynasty is often compared to the ancient Qin dynasty because both united China and were short-lived. The first Sui ruler, Yang Jiang, was also an ambitious ruler in the mold of the First Emperor. Yang Jiang had the Great Wall rebuilt and began an enormous construction project of his own. This was the Grand Canal, which linked the Yangtze River in the south to the Yellow River in the north.

THE LATE EMPIRE

The Tang dynasty, which then took control, had some similarities to the ancient Han government. Like the Han, the Tang rulers extended the borders of China. They also encouraged trade, which opened up the empire to new products and ideas from foreign lands. Under Tang rule, China became the wealthiest empire in the world.

Tang was a glorious time for the arts. During this dynasty, many of the finest Chinese paintings and poems were produced. This culturally rich period saw three of China's most important contributions to the world: the invention of a formula for gunpowder, the development of porcelain, and the production of the first printed book.

Severely weakened by rebellion, the Tang dynasty fell in 907. After several decades of unrest, the Song dynasty (960–1279) took its place. Ruling for more than three hundred years, the Song oversaw significant advances in technology, including the use of gunpowder in battle. Song dynasty artists were renowned for their landscape paintings, which depicted the natural world as a soothing retreat from everyday concerns.

In 1279, Mongol invaders from the north completed the conquest of China begun by Genghis Khan half a century earlier. Genghis Khan's grandson Kublai became the first emperor of the Yuan dynasty (1279–1368). He also became the first foreigner to rule all of China. The emperor encouraged trade along the Silk Road created in ancient times.

The Yuan dynasty was overthrown by a peasant army led by Buddhist monk Zhu Yuanzhang.

Tang artisans produced many beautiful statues and sculptures.

A REMARKABLE BEAN

The soybean, one of the healthiest foods for people to eat, was first cultivated in the eastern half of northern China in about the eleventh century BCE. It is one of the five main plant foods grown in China, along with rice, wheat, barley, and millet. The soybean is a legume, a plant with seeds that grow in pods, such as peas, beans, lentils, and peanuts. Soy is a highly nutritious food and an excellent source of protein. In ancient China, soy was used both as a food and as an ingredient

in making medicines. Soybeans can be processed to make a wide variety of other nutritious foods such as soy milk, tofu, soybean meal, and various types of seasonings. Many people enjoy eating soybeans directly from their green pods, a food called *edamame* in Japanese. Soybeans must be cooked to be eaten—raw soybeans are poisonous to humans and many other animals.

As the first emperor of the new Ming dynasty (1368–1644), he strengthened the powers of the emperor's position and largely succeeded in gaining control over all aspects of the government. During the Ming period, artisans produced many fine porcelain objects.

China again came under foreign rule in 1644. It was taken over by the Manchus, from Manchuria, who established the Qing dynasty. During the Qing era, China had increased contact

The Mongols referred to Kublai Khan as Setsen Khan, which means "The Wise Khan."

Zhu Yuanzhang was also known as Hongwu.

with other nations, such as Great Britain, Germany, Russia, France, and Japan. These countries seized parts of Chinese territory. Many Chinese resented these foreigners. They also disliked their Manchu rulers. A rebellion beginning in 1911 not only drove the Manchu from power, but also ended China's imperial rule.

MODERN CHINA

In 1912, China became a **republic**. In a republic, the people, not a king or an emperor, hold the power. The new Chinese government faced great difficulties over the next few decades, including a brutal war with Japanese invaders and an internal struggle for power. After a four-year civil war, communist leader Mao Zedong gained control in 1949 and renamed the country the People's Republic of China.

Under **communism**, the Chinese people were treated harshly. Many critics of the government were killed, especially during the Cultural Revolution (1966–1976). In this period, Mao's government wanted to do away with what it considered old ways of thinking. Countless ancient artifacts were destroyed. The government also attacked ancient belief systems—including Confucianism, Daoism, and Buddhism—and tried to erase their influence on the Chinese people.

In recent decades, China has been very successful in improving economic conditions throughout the country. In fact, China

republic (ri-PUHB-lik) a form of government in which the people have the power to elect representatives who manage the government

communism (KAHM-yuh-niz-uhm) a way of organizing the economy of a country so that all the land, property, businesses, and resources belong to the government or community, and the profits are shared by all

now has the second-largest economy in the world, after the United States. It also exports more manufactured goods than any other nation. With the growth of manufacturing, many Chinese people have moved from rural areas to cities to work in factories. City dwellers now make up about half of the total population.

Mao Zedong brought communist rule to China in 1949.

ANCIENT CITIES AND SITES

Modern China is very different than the China of ancient times, but it remains strongly connected to its past. For example, the Chinese name for the Chinese people, *Han*, comes from the name of the Han dynasty. The name *China* probably comes from the name of the Qin dynasty.

Modern China's precise boundaries have changed, but the country has been united since the third century BCE. And although China has seen periods of internal conflict and disunity, the Chinese consider themselves the oldest continuous civilization on Earth.

During the Cultural Revolution, posters of Mao Zedong were hung throughout the nation's cities.

Today, China has the largest population of any country.

Many Chinese people are now residents of cities that existed in the ancient world. Hangzhou, Nanjing, Suzhou, and Yangzhou have histories stretching back into ancient times. Luoyang has been occupied for about three thousand years. It served as the capital city of many emperors, including those of the Zhou, Han, and Tang dynasties.

Throughout much of the country, people have reminders of ancient China literally in their own backyards. Archaeological scholarship on China has exploded in recent years as more and more sites are discovered and excavated. Of course, some ancient artifacts are aboveground for all to see. The Great Wall, one of China's greatest engineering accomplishments, for example, has become a major tourist attraction for visitors from around the world.

Modern tourists visit a Tang period Buddhist cave temple in Luoyang.

ARTISTIC TREASURES

Tourists can now see ancient Chinese art at the renovated National Museum of China, which opened in Beijing in 2011. The museum has been criticized for ignoring controversial historical events, such as the Cultural Revolution. But it does show the government's increasing interest in promoting, rather than destroying, China's heritage. About one-quarter of the enormous museum is devoted to displaying artifacts and ancient art. Another celebrated museum of ancient Chinese art is the Shanghai Museum.

Even without visiting China, many people can see similar treasures. Museum collections on every continent feature

wondrous Chinese artifacts and artwork such as oracle bones, bronze vessels, jade ornaments, pottery, and lacquerware.

INVENTIONS AND BELIEFS

In China and beyond, people owe thanks to the ancient Chinese for their many great innovations and inventions. They introduced to the world common objects and materials such as paper, compasses, silk, and porcelain.

The National Museum of China is one of the world's largest museums.

Certain cultural practices of the ancient Chinese have also become widespread. In many countries, Chinese immigrants have popularized foods, spices, and cooking methods used in China for thousands of years. Traditional Chinese herbal medicines and acupuncture have gained wide acceptance as well. And each year, people living in cities with large Chinese populations take to the streets to watch elaborate Chinese New Year celebrations.

Chinese food is popular all around the world.

The intellectual traditions of ancient China have had an enormous impact around the globe. Scholars and spiritual seekers study Confucius and his teachings. In China, Confucian principles are still held dear. In recent years, many schools have begun to teach children as young as three about this ancient philosophy.

More and more Chinese people are participating in ancient religions, such as Buddhism.

Many Chinese people are also rediscovering Daoism and Buddhism. The communist government wanted to end all religious practices in China. But as the Chinese work to make sense of the modern world, they are increasingly returning to these traditional beliefs.

CELEBRATING CHINA'S HISTORY

With each generation, the literature of ancient China finds new readers. Modern translations of Laozi's *Daodejing* and Sunzi's

The Art of War keep these classics alive for readers from all cultures. Although ancient China's historians are not as widely read outside China, the men and women described in their works have frequently found a new home in other media.

For instance, the First Emperor remains a popular character. He has appeared in everything from operas to television shows. Although he has often been shown as a villain in China, the internationally famous Chinese filmmaker Zhang Yimou invited a reexamination of the First Emperor in *Hero* (2002). In the movie, he is presented as an honorable leader making hard choices for the good of his realm.

Cao Cao (155–220), a Han dynasty military leader and politician, is another ancient Chinese figure who has found a second life in popular culture. In China, he is best known from the fourteenth-century classic historical novel *Romance of the Three Kingdoms*. He has been the subject of many popular movies, TV shows, video games, and even a Japanese comic book series.

The Art of War *has been translated into many languages.*

In 2009, the discovery of what was thought to be Cao Cao's tomb made news worldwide. China's excitement was so great that in 2010, the opening of the tomb was broadcast live on national television. The event fizzled when it was revealed that robbers had raided the tomb. But the people of Xigaoxue village where the tomb was located, were still thrilled by the discovery.

The residents there enjoyed having a personal connection with one of the best-known figures from ancient times. But they

Hero, a film telling a story surrounding the First Emperor, was popular in many countries outside of China.

弘 扬 民 族 传 统 文 化

were equally enthusiastic about plans for the construction of a cultural relics theme park in the village. As one resident told *USA Today*, "This is a poor place, where we rely on the land, but now we hope to get rich from Cao Cao."

In this way, Xigaoxue mirrors China as a whole. A modern country looking both forward and backward, it is a place where the ancient past lives on in the present and future, sometimes in unexpected ways.

The excavation of Cao Cao's tomb turned out to be a major disappointment.

BIOGRAPHIES

BAN ZHAO (CA. 45–120 CE) was ancient China's most important female writer. She was the author of *Nü Jie* (*Lessons for Women*), a book of advice about how women should behave. She also finished her brother Ban Gu's history book, *Hanshu* (*History of the Former Han*), a history inspired by Sima Qian's work.

CAO CAO (155–220 CE) was a poet and a general. He was the most powerful man in the final years of the Han period. His son Cao Pi was the first emperor of the Wei dynasty.

CONFUCIUS (551–479 BCE) was a teacher of the Zhou period. He preached a philosophy that had a profound effect on both ancient and modern China. Confucianism values honesty, decency, strong ties to one's family, and obedience to one's ruler.

HAN WUDI (ALSO KNOWN AS EMPEROR WU) (156–87 BCE) nearly doubled the size of the Chinese empire through aggressive military campaigns. He also established an academy for civil servants that focused on the works of Confucius.

LAOZI (SIXTH CENTURY BCE) was the author of *Daodejing*, according to legend. This book of sayings became the basis for the philosophy of Daoism.

LIU BANG (CA. 256–195 BCE) led a rebellion against the second Qin emperor. After a bloody civil war, he established the Han dynasty and became its first emperor.

QIN SHI HUANGDI ("FIRST EMPEROR OF QIN") (259–210 BCE) founded the Qin dynasty in 221. He was the first ruler of the ancient Chinese empire.

Qu Yuan (339–278 BCE) wrote beautiful poetry after being sent into exile. His poems were later collected in the classic text *Songs of Chu*.

Sima Qian (CA. 145–CA. 90 BCE) was the most celebrated of all Chinese historians. He wrote the *Shiji* (*Historical Records*). This book was a history of China up to his time, and it became the model for later Chinese histories.

Sunzi (ALSO KNOWN AS SUN-TZU) (CA. FIFTH CENTURY BCE) was a general in the Chinese army. He is said to be the author of *Ping-fa* (*The Art of War*). This classic military manual includes strategies for understanding one's enemies and for defeating them on the battlefield.

Zhang Ling (34–156 CE) saw a vision of Laozi, the author of *Daodejing*, in 142. He subsequently established a new religion based on the philosophy of Daoism.

TIMELINE

CA. 2000–CA. 1600 BCE: *Traditional dates for the Xia dynasty.*

CA. 1200 BCE: *Anyang becomes the capital of the Shang kingdom.*

7000	2000	1000

CA. 7000 BCE: *Humans begin to farm in what becomes present-day China.*

CA. 1600–CA. 1050 BCE: *Traditional dates for the Shang dynasty.*

CA. 1050–771 BCE: *The Western Zhou period, the first part of the Zhou dynasty.*

771 BCE: *The Zhou ruler You is assassinated, and his son establishes a new Zhou capital to the east, in present-day Luoyang.*

771–221 BCE: *The Eastern Zhou period, the latter part of the Zhou dynasty, when the Zhou kings had very little real power.*

771–475 BCE: *The Spring and Autumn period, the first half of the Eastern Zhou period, which sees great unrest and instability.*

210 BCE: *Qin Shi Huangdi (the First Emperor), who united the warring states into the Chinese empire, dies.*

141 BCE: *Han Wudi becomes emperor and begins overseeing a major expansion of the Chinese empire.*

FIRST CENTURY BCE: *Chinese historian Sima Qian writes Shiji (Historical Records).*

500

0

278 BCE: *Famed Chinese poet Qu Yuan commits suicide.*

CA. FIFTH CENTURY BCE: *Military leader Sunzi writes The Art of War.*

475–221 BCE: *The Warring States period, the second half of the Eastern Zhou period, which witnesses the division of China into seven hostile states.*

CA. SIXTH CENTURY BCE: *Laozi writes Daodejing, the basis for the philosophy of Daoism.*

551 BCE: *Chinese philosopher-thinker Confucius is born.*

142 CE: *Zhang Ling has a vision of Laozi, which inspires a Daoism-based religious movement.*

220–265 CE: *The Wei dynasty rules.*

265–316 CE: *The Jin dynasty rules.*

500

1000

618–907 CE: *The Tang dynasty rules.*

581– 618 CE: *The Sui dynasty rules.*

1279 CE: *Kublai Khan completes the conquest of China.*

1279–1368 CE: *The Yuan dynasty rules.*

960–1279 CE: *The Song dynasty rules.*

1644–1911 CE: *The Qing dynasty rules.*

2010 CE: *The opening of the tomb of Cao Cao, a Han military and political leader, is broadcast live on Chinese television.*

2011 CE: *The renovated National Museum of China, featuring a huge display of ancient Chinese artifacts, opens in Beijing.*

1500

2000

1974 CE: *The terra-cotta sculpture army is found near the tomb of the First Emperor.*

1966–1976 CE: *Chairman Mao tries to eliminate ties to traditional Chinese culture and beliefs during the Cultural Revolution.*

1949 CE: *Mao Zedong establishes communist rule over what is now the People's Republic of China.*

1368–1644 CE: *The Ming dynasty rules.*

1912 CE: *The Chinese overthrow the Qing dynasty, and China becomes a republic.*

GLOSSARY

alchemists (AL-kuh-mists) people who work to make a potion that gives eternal youth or who try to change common metals into gold

artifacts (AHR-tuh-fakts) objects made or changed by human beings, especially tools or weapons used in the past

artisans (AHR-ti-zuhnz) people who are skilled at working with their hands at a particular craft

civil service (SIV-uhl SUR-vis) an organization of officials who administer a government's policies

communism (KAHM-yuh-niz-uhm) a way of organizing the economy of a country so that all the land, property, businesses, and resources belong to the government or community, and the profits are shared by all

concubine (KONG-kyu-bine) a woman who lives with a man but is not married to him

currency (KUR-uhn-see) the form of money used in a country

descendants (di-SEN-duhnts) a person's children, their children, and so on into the future

drought (DROUT) a long period without rain

dynasty (DYE-nuh-stee) a series of rulers belonging to the same family

excavated (EK-skuh-vay-tid) dug from the earth, often at an archaeological site

famine (FAM-in) a shortage of food causing starvation in a geographical area

imperial (im-PEER-ee-uhl) of or having to do with an empire

inscriptions (in-SKRIP-shuhnz) words carved or written on an object

lacquer (LAK-kur) the sap of the lac tree used as a varnish

mandate (MAN-date) a command or authorization

monsoons (MAHN-soonz) very strong winds; in summer they blow from the ocean, causing heavy rains; in winter they blow toward the ocean, creating hot, dry weather

porcelain (POR-suh-lin) very fine pottery, often called "china" by Europeans

prose (PROZE) ordinary written or spoken language, as opposed to verse or poetry

reforms (ri-FORMZ) improvements or corrections of something unsatisfactory

reincarnation (ree-in-kahr-NAY-shuhn) being born on Earth again in another body after dying

republic (ri-PUHB-lik) a form of government in which the people have the power to elect representatives who manage the government

ritual (RICH-oo-uhl) an act or series of acts that are always performed in the same way, usually as part of a religious or social ceremony

successor (suhk-SES-ur) one person who follows another in a position or sequence

FIND OUT MORE

BOOKS

Hoobler, Dorothy, and Thomas Hoobler. *Confucianism.*
New York: Chelsea House, 2009.

Roberts, Jeremy. *Chinese Mythology A to Z.*
New York: Chelsea House, 2010.

Schomp, Virginia. *The Ancient Chinese.* New York:
Marshall Cavendish Benchmark, 2009.

Shaughnessy, Edward L. *Exploring the Life, Myth, and Art of
Ancient China.* New York: Rosen Publishing Group, 2009.

Whitfield, Susan. *Philosophy and Writing.*
Armonk, NY: Sharpe Focus, 2009.

Visit this Scholastic Web site for more
information on Ancient China:
www.factsfornow.scholastic.com
Enter the keywords **Ancient China**

INDEX

Page numbers in *italics* indicate a photograph or map.

ABOUT THE AUTHOR

A graduate of Swarthmore College, Liz Sonneborn is a full-time writer living in Brooklyn, New York. She has written more than ninety nonfiction books for both children and adults on a wide variety of subjects. Her works include *The Egyptians, The Romans, The Ancient Aztecs,* and *The Ancient Kushites,* the last of which was named an Honor Book by the African Studies Association's Children's Africana Book Awards.